Wishes, Advice, and Happy Thoughts for

BABY

and _____ from us

Additional Wishes, Advice, and Happy Thoughts

_____

_____

_____

_____

_____

_____

_____

_____

I love thinking about how

_____

you'll be with your baby.

With love, _____

Additional Wishes, Advice, and Happy Thoughts

_____

_____

_____

_____

_____

_____

_____

_____

I hope your baby always appreciates your

_____ .

With love, _____

Additional Wishes, Advice, and Happy Thoughts

When the baby sleeps, remember to

_____ .

With love, _____

Additional Wishes, Advice, and Happy Thoughts

_____

_____

_____

_____

_____

_____

_____

_____

If you need me to, I'll always

_____ .

With love, _____

Additional Wishes, Advice, and Happy Thoughts

_____

_____

_____

_____

_____

_____

_____

_____

Baby might be a champion at

_____ .

With love, _____

Additional Wishes, Advice, and Happy Thoughts

Let's call your baby

" _____ "

——————————————————————— .

With love, _____

Additional Wishes, Advice, and Happy Thoughts

I hope we can

_____

with your baby.

With love, _____

Additional Wishes, Advice, and Happy Thoughts

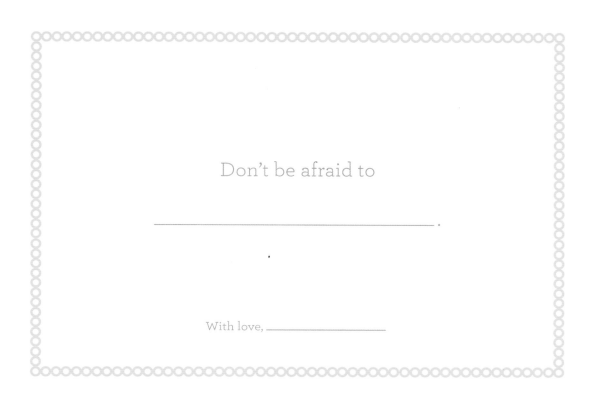

Don't be afraid to

_____ .

.

With love, _____

Additional Wishes, Advice, and Happy Thoughts

Wouldn't it be great if your baby never

_____ ?

With love, _____

Additional Wishes, Advice, and Happy Thoughts

Wouldn't it be great if your baby always

_____?

With love, _____

Additional Wishes, Advice, and Happy Thoughts

_____

_____

_____

_____

_____

_____

_____

I hope the baby gets your

_____ .

With love, _____

Additional Wishes, Advice, and Happy Thoughts

_____

with your baby is going to be the best.

With love, _____

Additional Wishes, Advice, and Happy Thoughts

_____

_____

_____

_____

_____

_____

_____

_____

I hope your baby laughs at

_____ .

With love, _____

Additional Wishes, Advice, and Happy Thoughts

_____

_____

_____

_____

_____

_____

_____

_____

When you're tired, remember that

_____ .

With love, _____

Additional Wishes, Advice, and Happy Thoughts

Baby's first year will probably be

_____ .

With love, _____

Additional Wishes, Advice, and Happy Thoughts

_____

_____

_____

_____

_____

_____

_____

_____

_____

_____

I'll bet your baby will grow up to be

_____ .

With love, _____

Additional Wishes, Advice, and Happy Thoughts

_____

_____

_____

_____

_____

_____

_____

_____

Make sure to always keep

_____

in your diaper bag.

With love, _____

Additional Wishes, Advice, and Happy Thoughts

I can't wait to

_____

with the baby.

With love, _____

Additional Wishes, Advice, and Happy Thoughts

I hope your baby learns to

_____ .

With love, _____

Additional Wishes, Advice, and Happy Thoughts

Don't forget to

_____ .

With love, _____

Additional Wishes, Advice, and Happy Thoughts

Your baby will probably be amazing at

_____ .

With love, _____

Additional Wishes, Advice, and Happy Thoughts

I hope your baby wears

_____ .

With love, _____

Additional Wishes, Advice, and Happy Thoughts

We're going to have so much fun

_____

with baby.

With love, _____

Additional Wishes, Advice, and Happy Thoughts

It is so

_____

to watch you

_____

With love, _____

Additional Wishes, Advice, and Happy Thoughts

Don't leave home without

_____ .

With love, _____

Additional Wishes, Advice, and Happy Thoughts

_____

_____

_____

_____

_____

_____

_____

_____

Never underestimate your

_____

as a mom.

With love, _____

Additional Wishes, Advice, and Happy Thoughts

It's perfectly okay to

_____ .

With love, _____

Additional Wishes, Advice, and Happy Thoughts

This baby is so lucky to have

_____ .

With love, _____

Additional Wishes, Advice, and Happy Thoughts

_____

_____

_____

_____

_____

_____

_____

Trust your

_____ .

With love, _____

Additional Wishes, Advice, and Happy Thoughts

_____

_____

_____

_____

_____

_____

_____

_____

Don't listen to anyone who tells you to

_____ .

With love, _____

Additional Wishes, Advice, and Happy Thoughts

I wish nothing but

_____

for your family.

With love, _____

Additional Wishes, Advice, and Happy Thoughts

I want to hear all about your baby's

_____ .

With love, _____

Additional Wishes, Advice, and Happy Thoughts

Maybe your baby will love

_____

as much as you do.

With love, _____

Additional Wishes, Advice, and Happy Thoughts

I can't wait to see what happens when

_____ .

With love, _____

Additional Wishes, Advice, and Happy Thoughts

When the baby is

_____ ,

try

_____ .

With love, _____

Additional Wishes, Advice, and Happy Thoughts

_____

_____

_____

_____

_____

_____

_____

_____

Your baby might look like a mini

_____ .

With love, _____

Additional Wishes, Advice, and Happy Thoughts

On hard days, remember to

_____.

With love, _____

Additional Wishes, Advice, and Happy Thoughts

_____

_____

_____

_____

_____

_____

_____

_____

Your baby will be so

_____ .

With love, _____

Additional Wishes, Advice, and Happy Thoughts

_____

_____

_____

_____

_____

_____

_____

_____

After the baby arrives, I hope you get to

_____ .

With love, _____

Additional Wishes, Advice, and Happy Thoughts

_____

_____

_____

_____

_____

_____

_____

_____

You're going to be the

_____

mom ever.

With love, _____

Welcome, baby

_____!

We can't wait to meet you.

Guests:

_____   _____
_____   _____
_____   _____
_____   _____
_____   _____
_____   _____
_____   _____
_____   _____
_____   _____
_____   _____
_____   _____

Gifts:

Guests:

Gifts:

_____   _____
_____   _____
_____   _____
_____   _____
_____   _____
_____   _____
_____   _____
_____   _____
_____   _____
_____   _____

Guests:

Gifts:

Fill in the *Love*.

Created, published, and distributed by Knock Knock
1635-B Electric Ave.
Venice, CA 90291
knockknockstuff.com
Knock Knock is a registered trademark of Knock Knock LLC
Fill in the Love is a registered trademark of Knock Knock LLC

ISBN: 978-160106919-1
UPC: 825703-50233-6
10 9 8 7 6 5 4 3